EXPLORING SPACE

ROVERS AND LANDERS

BY DALTON RAINS

WWW.APEXEDITIONS.COM

Copyright © 2024 by Apex Editions, Mendota Heights, MN 55120. All rights reserved. No part of this book may be reproduced or utilized in any form or by any means without written permission from the publisher.

Apex is distributed by North Star Editions:
sales@northstareditions.com | 888-417-0195

Produced for Apex by Red Line Editorial.

Photographs ©: NASA, cover, 1, 4–5, 7, 8, 9, 10–11, 13, 14, 15, 18–19, 20–21, 22–23, 24, 29; Science History Images/Alamy, 12; NASA TV/AP Images, 16–17; ESA/SIPA/AP Images, 25; Kyodo/Newscom, 26

Library of Congress Control Number: 2023910085

ISBN
978-1-63738-741-2 (hardcover)
978-1-63738-784-9 (paperback)
978-1-63738-869-3 (ebook pdf)
978-1-63738-827-3 (hosted ebook)

Printed in the United States of America
Mankato, MN
012024

NOTE TO PARENTS AND EDUCATORS

Apex books are designed to build literacy skills in striving readers. Exciting, high-interest content attracts and holds readers' attention. The text is carefully leveled to allow students to achieve success quickly. Additional features, such as bolded glossary words for difficult terms, help build comprehension.

TABLE OF CONTENTS

CHAPTER 1
PERSEVERANCE 4

CHAPTER 2
EARLY MISSIONS 10

CHAPTER 3
EXPLORING MARS 16

CHAPTER 4
MORE MISSIONS 22

COMPREHENSION QUESTIONS • 28
GLOSSARY • 30
TO LEARN MORE • 31
ABOUT THE AUTHOR • 31
INDEX • 32

CHAPTER 1

PERSEVERANCE

A spacecraft falls toward Mars. It uses a parachute. That helps it slow down. Then the ship releases its **heat shield**.

Scientists test *Perseverance*'s parachute in 2017.

The spacecraft uses its rockets. The rockets help it fly closer to the surface. Part of the spacecraft separates. It lowers the *Perseverance* rover to the ground with wires.

FAST FACT

Perseverance landed in a large crater. Scientists believe the crater once held a lake.

Perseverance landed on Mars in February 2021.

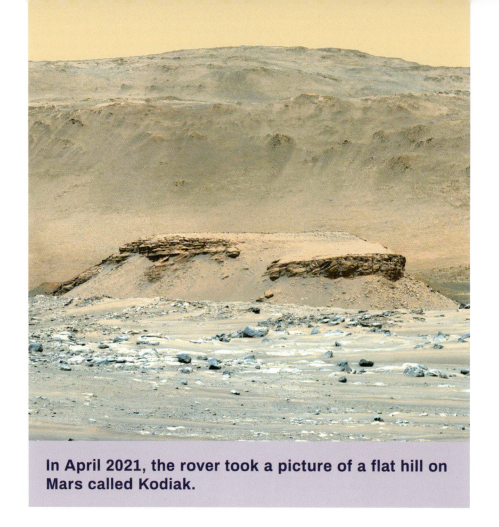

In April 2021, the rover took a picture of a flat hill on Mars called Kodiak.

Soon, the rover begins to study Mars. It takes many pictures. It uses a drill, too. The drill helps the rover gather rocks and soil **samples**.

SLOW MOVING

Perseverance has rechargeable batteries. It uses a small power system to charge them. The rover moves very slowly. That helps it use less energy.

Perseverance's drill goes into the ground. Then it takes samples that are circle shaped.

CHAPTER 2

EARLY MISSIONS

A rover is a type of space **vehicle**. It moves around land. A lander is different. It goes to the ground. But it does not move around.

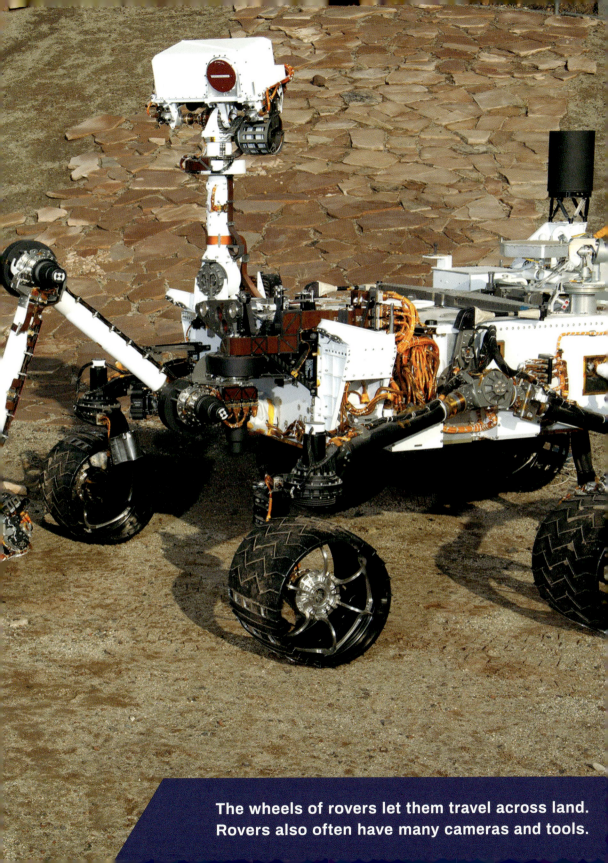

The wheels of rovers let them travel across land. Rovers also often have many cameras and tools.

The Soviet Union was the first country to send a rover to the Moon.

In 1969, **astronauts** traveled to the Moon. They went down to the surface in a lander. The next year, the first rover reached the Moon.

VENUS

The **Soviet Union** sent landers to Venus. The first one went there in 1970. The lander worked for more than 20 minutes. It sent measurements back to Earth.

The surface of Venus is about 900 degrees Fahrenheit (475°C).

The *Viking 1* lander weighed 1,261 pounds (572 kg).

Scientists wanted to land on Mars next. They built two landers. They were *Viking 1* and *Viking 2*. Both reached Mars in 1976. The landers took pictures. They also looked for signs of life.

FAST FACT
The Viking landers took nearly a year to travel from Earth to Mars.

A rocket launched the *Viking 1* lander on August 20, 1975.

CHAPTER 3

EXPLORING MARS

Scientists learned a lot about Mars from landers. But they wanted to know even more. So, they decided to send a rover. The first one landed on Mars in 1997.

16

The first rover on Mars was *Sojourner*. It worked for 83 days.

Next, the United States sent two more rovers to Mars. *Spirit* and *Opportunity* landed in 2004. They searched for signs of water.

Opportunity took photos and gathered data on Mars for nearly 15 years.

AMAZING AIRBAGS

Some early rovers used **airbags** to land safely. They filled with air right before the landers hit the surface. The landers bounced on the ground. But the airbags protected them.

The rovers examined the areas where they landed. *Opportunity* found **minerals** formed by water. It helped prove that Mars once had water.

Opportunity found minerals in a valley called Mawrth Vallis.

FAST FACT
Spirit explored Mars until 2010. Opportunity worked until 2018.

CHAPTER 4

MORE MISSIONS

Scientists continued to learn about the **solar system**. The Curiosity rover landed on Mars in 2012. It explored a crater. The rover tested rocks and soil.

By 2023, *Curiosity* had traveled more than 18 miles (29 km) on Mars.

Perseverance carried the *Ingenuity* helicopter. It made the first powered, controlled flight on a different planet.

Perseverance arrived on Mars in 2021. The rover went to new places. It also tested technology for future missions.

Philae took close-up pictures of a comet.

COOL COMET

Philae landed on a **comet**. It was the first lander to do so. It studied gas and dust there. The lander took pictures, too.

Scientists planned more missions for the future. They hoped to retrieve samples from *Perseverance*. They planned to study the samples back on Earth.

FAST FACT
In 2023, several countries were planning missions. Some wanted to explore one of Mars's moons.

◀ In 2021, a company in Japan showed off its tiny rover. *YAOKI* weighed about 1.1 pounds (0.5 kg).

COMPREHENSION QUESTIONS

Write your answers on a separate piece of paper.

1. Write a few sentences that explain the main ideas of Chapter 3.

2. Which rover do you find most interesting? Why?

3. What was the first mission to land on Mars?

    A. Viking 1
    B. Perseverance
    C. Philae

4. How long did the *Opportunity* rover explore Mars?

    A. 6 years
    B. 14 years
    C. 40 years

5. What does **examined** mean in this book?

The rovers examined the areas where they landed. Opportunity *found minerals formed by water.*

    A. looked at closely
    B. drove away from
    C. dug large holes in

6. What does **retrieve** mean in this book?

They hoped to retrieve samples from Perseverance. They planned to study the samples back on Earth.

    A. get or bring something back
    B. destroy or throw away
    C. move underground

Answer key on page 32.

GLOSSARY

airbags
Bags that quickly fill with air and are used as cushions.

astronauts
People who are trained to travel in a spacecraft.

comet
A large object made of dust and ice that circles the Sun.

heat shield
A barrier that protects a spacecraft from heat.

minerals
Solid materials that occur in nature.

samples
Small amounts of a material that scientists collect and study.

solar system
An area that includes the Sun and all of the planets and other objects that move around it.

Soviet Union
A country in Europe and Asia that existed from 1922 to 1991.

vehicle
A machine that moves around.

BOOKS

Murray, Julie. *Rovers*. Minneapolis: Abdo Publishing, 2020.
Sommer, Nathan. *Mars*. Minneapolis: Bellwether Media, 2019.
Ventura, Marne. *The Planets*. Mendota Heights, MN: Focus Readers, 2023.

ONLINE RESOURCES

Visit **www.apexeditions.com** to find links and resources related to this title.

ABOUT THE AUTHOR

Dalton Rains is an author and editor from Saint Paul, Minnesota. He loves to learn about new science discoveries.

INDEX

B
batteries, 9

C
crater, 6, 22
Curiosity, 22

D
drill, 8

H
heat shield, 4

M
minerals, 20
Moon, 12

O
Opportunity, 18, 20–21

P
Perseverance, 4, 6, 8–9, 24, 27
Philae, 25
pictures, 8, 14, 25

R
rocks, 8, 22

S
samples, 8, 27
Spirit, 18, 21

V
Venus, 13
Viking landers, 14–15

W
water, 18, 20

ANSWER KEY:
1. Answers will vary; 2. Answers will vary; 3. A; 4. B; 5. A; 6. A